CW01431607

Original title:
Oblique Smoke Along the Faerie Turf

Copyright © 2025 Swan Charm
All rights reserved.

Author: Liina Liblikas
ISBN HARDBACK: 978-1-80562-633-6
ISBN PAPERBACK: 978-1-80564-154-4

Reflected Glory in the Velvet Night

The moon, a silver coin, so bright,
Casts shadows deep in velvet night.
Stars whisper tales of ages past,
While dreams like white doves soar fast.

A mirror in the lake below,
Reflecting worlds we yearn to know.
Beneath the branches, whispers swirl,
As twilight dances, shadows twirl.

In the silence, magic leaps,
Awakens secrets that night keeps.
With every glance, the cosmos sings,
Of whispered hopes and gentle things.

A symphony of night unfolds,
In hues of indigo and gold.
The heart of nature beats in time,
With every pulse, an echoing rhyme.

So linger in this sacred space,
Embrace the night, its warm embrace.
For in the dark, the light will shine,
Reflecting glory, pure and divine.

A Tapestry of Grace Beneath the Stars

In twilight's arms, a canvas spreads,
A tapestry where starlight threads.
Each twinkling point, a story spun,
Of lovers lost and battles won.

The heavens flaunt their shimmering lace,
As dreams descend in gentle grace.
The nightingale sings soft and low,
To guide the hearts that yearn to know.

Beneath this dome, the shadows play,
In fleeting forms that twist and sway.
Every breath, a whispered prayer,
A silent wish sent through the air.

With every breath, the heavens sigh,
Weaving wishes into the sky.
A dance of fate in cosmic rhyme,
Embracing all through space and time.

So let your heart be open wide,
To drift where dreams and starlight bide.
For in this grace, we find our place,
A tapestry where souls embrace.

Curious Shapes in the Wandering Night

Shapes emerge in the wandering night,
As shadows leap in playful flight.
Whispers of secrets in the dark,
Evoke the flames of a hidden spark.

The trees, they lean, with silent grace,
Guarding tales that time can't erase.
Each rustle, an echo of delight,
Curious shapes in the soft moonlight.

A fox darts through with a flick of its tail,
In search of paths where wild things trail.
Ghostly figures dance and glide,
In the soft embrace of the night outside.

Dreams unfold in cryptic forms,
Breathing life where magic warms.
Each twist of fate in endless flight,
Curious shapes, a wondrous sight.

So wander forth beneath the skies,
And gaze into the night's surprise.
For in the shapes that softly call,
The wandering night reveals it all.

A Tapestry of Grace Beneath the Stars

In twilight's arms, a canvas spreads,
A tapestry where starlight threads.
Each twinkling point, a story spun,
Of lovers lost and battles won.

The heavens flaunt their shimmering lace,
As dreams descend in gentle grace.
The nightingale sings soft and low,
To guide the hearts that yearn to know.

Beneath this dome, the shadows play,
In fleeting forms that twist and sway.
Every breath, a whispered prayer,
A silent wish sent through the air.

With every breath, the heavens sigh,
Weaving wishes into the sky.
A dance of fate in cosmic rhyme,
Embracing all through space and time.

So let your heart be open wide,
To drift where dreams and starlight bide.
For in this grace, we find our place,
A tapestry where souls embrace.

Curious Shapes in the Wandering Night

Shapes emerge in the wandering night,
As shadows leap in playful flight.
Whispers of secrets in the dark,
Evoke the flames of a hidden spark.

The trees, they lean, with silent grace,
Guarding tales that time can't erase.
Each rustle, an echo of delight,
Curious shapes in the soft moonlight.

A fox darts through with a flick of its tail,
In search of paths where wild things trail.
Ghostly figures dance and glide,
In the soft embrace of the night outside.

Dreams unfold in cryptic forms,
Breathing life where magic warms.
Each twist of fate in endless flight,
Curious shapes, a wondrous sight.

So wander forth beneath the skies,
And gaze into the night's surprise.
For in the shapes that softly call,
The wandering night reveals it all.

Radiant Dreams in the Lush Understories

In lush understories, shadows play,
Where sunlight dances, bright and gay.
The heart of the earth hums soft and low,
As radiant dreams begin to flow.

Ferns unfurl with a gentle sigh,
Filling the air, as breezes fly.
Every leaf, a soft-spoken wish,
Each petal drips with a timeless kiss.

Beneath the boughs, a world awakes,
With secrets deep and gentle breaks.
The nightingale's soft serenade,
Lulls the forest, in beauty laid.

In this refuge, dreams take flight,
Guided by stars, they find their light.
In whispers found where shadows dwell,
Radiant stories weave a spell.

So breathe in deep, let wonders glean,
Amidst the thrumming, lush and green.
For in the heart of nature's grace,
Radiant dreams find their place.

Luminous Veils Over Moonlit Mounds

Veils of silver drape the night,
Casting glow on mounds so bright.
Whispers dance on gentle breeze,
Wrapped in magic, hearts find ease.

Shadows play where secrets dwell,
In the silence, tales they tell.
Stars above their vigil keep,
Cradling dreams in tender sleep.

Mysterious paths lead us through,
To realms where wishes do come true.
With every step, the world awakes,
Beneath the moon, our laughter breaks.

Nature's song begins to rise,
A symphony beneath the skies.
Veils of light in twinkling grace,
Guide lost souls to their own place.

Fantasies Glimmering in the Dusk

In the dusk where wishes soar,
Fantasies knock on twilight's door.
Glistening dreams in colors bright,
Weaving wonders into night.

Beneath the trees, shadows hide,
Echoes of the heart's deep pride.
Sparks of hope in every rhyme,
Mark the passage of our time.

Gentle whispers call our name,
In this realm, we play the game.
With lightness, we shall embrace,
The fleeting waltz of time and space.

Elfin laughter fills the air,
Wings of magic everywhere.
Moments caught in sapphire nets,
In the dusk, no room for regrets.

Wisps of Enchantment in the Air

Enchantment swirls like morning mist,
Each soft breath a tender twist.
Whispers linger, secrets shared,
In the air, our dreams are bared.

Echoes of a melody,
Paint the sky, wild and free.
Every note a guiding star,
Leading us, no matter how far.

Through the fog, a flicker glows,
Bringing warmth when the cold wind blows.
In the depths of hidden glades,
Light reveals what dark forbade.

Dance with shadows, laugh with fire,
Awakening our deep desire.
In the night, we spin and sway,
Crafting dreams that won't decay.

Fantasies Glimmering in the Dusk

In the dusk where wishes soar,
Fantasies knock on twilight's door.
Glistening dreams in colors bright,
Weaving wonders into night.

Beneath the trees, shadows hide,
Echoes of the heart's deep pride.
Sparks of hope in every rhyme,
Mark the passage of our time.

Gentle whispers call our name,
In this realm, we play the game.
With lightness, we shall embrace,
The fleeting waltz of time and space.

Elfin laughter fills the air,
Wings of magic everywhere.
Moments caught in sapphire nets,
In the dusk, no room for regrets.

Wisps of Enchantment in the Air

Enchantment swirls like morning mist,
Each soft breath a tender twist.
Whispers linger, secrets shared,
In the air, our dreams are bared.

Echoes of a melody,
Paint the sky, wild and free.
Every note a guiding star,
Leading us, no matter how far.

Through the fog, a flicker glows,
Bringing warmth when the cold wind blows.
In the depths of hidden glades,
Light reveals what dark forbade.

Dance with shadows, laugh with fire,
Awakening our deep desire.
In the night, we spin and sway,
Crafting dreams that won't decay.

The Breath of Mirage Beneath the Stars

Mirages drift in starry streams,
Filling our hearts with silent dreams.
Each shimmering thread woven tight,
Glows with the magic of the night.

The moon's soft gaze, a beacon bright,
Guiding wanderers lost in flight.
In the stillness, spirits dance,
Entwined in a timeless romance.

Underneath the celestial dome,
Every heart begins to roam.
Wishes whispered on the wind,
Lost and found, our souls rescind.

Here, the night breathes with delight,
Crafting wonders out of sight.
In each heartbeat, magic flows,
Sowing seeds where love still grows.

Mirage of the Sparkling Ethereal Sea

In dreams where whispers dance and play,
The sea shimmers with hues of gray.
A horizon kissed by twilight's breath,
Echoes linger of life and death.

Waves of silver, secrets unspun,
Chasing the light of the sinking sun.
A mirage beckons, laced in mist,
Promises linger, too sweet to resist.

Footprints vanish in shimmering foam,
Songs of the deep call you to roam.
With each pulse of the tide's embrace,
Lost in the depths of this timeless place.

Stars begin to twinkle, faint and bold,
Stories of sailors and fortunes told.
In the heart of the sea, dreams weave,
Treasures await those who believe.

Yet as dawn breaks, the magic fades,
A fleeting glimpse through nature's charades.
The sea's lullaby, a soft goodbye,
Echoes the truth, with a gentle sigh.

The Breath of Mirage Beneath the Stars

Mirages drift in starry streams,
Filling our hearts with silent dreams.
Each shimmering thread woven tight,
Glows with the magic of the night.

The moon's soft gaze, a beacon bright,
Guiding wanderers lost in flight.
In the stillness, spirits dance,
Entwined in a timeless romance.

Underneath the celestial dome,
Every heart begins to roam.
Wishes whispered on the wind,
Lost and found, our souls rescind.

Here, the night breathes with delight,
Crafting wonders out of sight.
In each heartbeat, magic flows,
Sowing seeds where love still grows.

Mirage of the Sparkling Ethereal Sea

In dreams where whispers dance and play,
The sea shimmers with hues of gray.
A horizon kissed by twilight's breath,
Echoes linger of life and death.

Waves of silver, secrets unspun,
Chasing the light of the sinking sun.
A mirage beckons, laced in mist,
Promises linger, too sweet to resist.

Footprints vanish in shimmering foam,
Songs of the deep call you to roam.
With each pulse of the tide's embrace,
Lost in the depths of this timeless place.

Stars begin to twinkle, faint and bold,
Stories of sailors and fortunes told.
In the heart of the sea, dreams weave,
Treasures await those who believe.

Yet as dawn breaks, the magic fades,
A fleeting glimpse through nature's charades.
The sea's lullaby, a soft goodbye,
Echoes the truth, with a gentle sigh.

The Twilight's Silent Serenade

In the hush of dusk, where shadows blend,
The twilight sings, a hushed commend.
With violets and gold in the sky's embrace,
Lullabies linger, calm and grace.

Trees stand tall, bathed in a glow,
Their whispers soft, stories flow.
As fireflies waltz in the cooling air,
A dance of light, beyond compare.

The world grows quiet, the stars awake,
Silver paths upon the lake.
Each ripple carries a soothing sound,
Echoes of love, profound and unbound.

Moonlight spills like a silken thread,
Stitching the night as day has fled.
A serenade of silence sings,
Nature's orchestra, in slumber it clings.

In twilight's arms, dreams take flight,
A ballet performed in the soft moonlight.
As night unfolds its velvet cloak,
Whispers of wonder softly spoke.

Glimmers in the Glooming Wood

In woods where shadows twist and sway,
A glimmer shines through night and day.
Mossy carpets underfoot,
A treasure hidden, lost yet astute.

Ancient trees with twisted limbs,
Hushed secrets of forgotten hymns.
Amidst the gloom, fireflies gleam,
A light to guide the wandering dream.

Branches beckon, whisper low,
A siren call, soft as snow.
Echoes of laughter, faint and warm,
Resound in the heart, a vivid charm.

Each step reveals a world anew,
Shaded paths where magic grew.
Glimmers bright as the night descends,
A waltz of wonders that never ends.

So linger here, seek quiet grace,
In the tranquil depths of this hallowed place.
For in the gloom, light finds its way,
In loving whispers where shadows play.

Reverie of Whimsical Shadows

In a realm where shadows waltz and sway,
Whispers of magic begin to play.
Shapes in the dark twist with delight,
A reverie crafted by the night.

With colors spilled from a painter's dream,
Fantastical visions in soft moonbeam.
Each shadow tells a tale once spun,
Of creatures that dance when the day is done.

Laughter drifts through the velvet gloom,
As starlight blooms in every room.
Curious figures flicker and tease,
In a playful land where hearts find ease.

Through the canvas of night they weave and twine,
Whimsical echoes, a world divine.
In this reverie, let spirits soar,
A dream-stitched life forevermore.

As dawn approaches, the shadows fade,
Yet in our hearts, their song is laid.
Awake to the magic that lingers near,
In the whispering shadows, the dreams appear.

Phantoms of Wonder Across the Meadow

In whispers soft, the grasses sway,
With secrets kept of yesterday.
Beneath the sky, where dreams may roam,
The phantoms dance, forever home.

Their laughter glimmers in the breeze,
As twilight weaves between the trees.
With every step, the echoes call,
A spellbound world that holds us all.

The meadow holds its silent grace,
Where shadows play, and spirits chase.
With hearts unbound, we boldly leap,
Into the magic, vast and deep.

Through petals bright and streams that sing,
The essence of the fey takes wing.
In twilight's glow, our souls ignite,
A tapestry of pure delight.

As stars awaken, secrets gleam,
In nature's heart, our spirits dream.
In phantoms' arms, forever free,
We'll wander through eternity.

Echoes of Laughter in Cosmic Fogs

In cosmic veils, the laughter flies,
Beneath the vast and starry skies.
With joyful notes that softly blend,
These echoes whisper, never end.

The fogs arise and twirl around,
In shimmering hues, they dance unbound.
Each twinkling star a secret shared,
Of fleeting dreams that were once dared.

With every giggle, worlds ignite,
A symphony of purest light.
Where shadows roam and spirits play,
In cosmic myths, we find our way.

From nebulae of magic spun,
We chase the glow of every sun.
In giggling tides, we drift along,
United in a cosmic song.

Each heartbeat echoes through the fog,
As starlit memories softly cog.
The laughter lingers, never lost,
In cosmic dreams, we pay the cost.

Silhouettes in the Radiant Twilight

In radiant hues, the silhouettes rise,
Dancing softly 'neath fading skies.
With every breath, the twilight gleams,
As shadows weave their whispered dreams.

The horizon blushes, a soft embrace,
While memories linger in this place.
With hands outstretched, we greet the night,
A canvas painted with pure light.

The whispers of dusk hold tales untold,
Of adventures chasing shadows bold.
In twilight's glow, our hearts align,
With every beat, our fates entwine.

Through every corner of the dark,
The silhouettes leave their magic mark.
As stars awake, our spirits soar,
In radiant twilight, we crave more.

From dusk till dawn, we dare to dream,
As life unfolds like a silken seam.
In this embrace of dark and bright,
We find our truth in the giving light.

Mists That Bind the Heart's Secrets

In morning mists, the secrets lie,
Wrapped in whispers, a gentle sigh.
With every breath, the shadows drift,
A binding magic, a hidden gift.

Through tangled woods, the echoes call,
With quiet eyes that see it all.
As tendrils curl around the trees,
Our heart's confessions find their ease.

The mists enfold each whispered word,
In silent vows, our thoughts are heard.
With every step, the dangers fade,
In mystery's arms, we are unmade.

A dance of spirits through the dawn,
Where dreams awaken, gently drawn.
In every sigh, the truth ignites,
A bond that weaves through endless nights.

In shadows deep, we learn to trust,
This fleeting world of fog and dust.
The secrets bind, forever near,
In mists that cradle all we hold dear.

Whispers of Gossamer Veils

In the shimmer of twilight's grace,
Veils of whispers softly trace.
Secrets dance in the gentle breeze,
Nature hums with tender ease.

Stars begin their nightly show,
Casting glimmers down below.
Each flicker tells a tale of old,
In patterns woven, dreams unfold.

Beneath the boughs of ancient trees,
Where shadows play and spirits tease,
A lullaby hangs in the air,
Calling souls to linger there.

Moonlight spills on velvet ground,
Every heartbeat, a magic sound.
Enchantment twirls in soft embrace,
Time slips by without a trace.

With gossamer threads the night is spun,
Underneath the watching sun.
In echoes of the velvet night,
We find our hearts in whispered light.

Enigmatic Echoes in Midnight Mist

Through the shroud of lingering mist,
Echoes murmur, softly kissed.
Voices rise from the depths of dreams,
Weaving spells in silver streams.

Beneath the watchful, twinkling skies,
Mysteries linger, love never dies.
Each shadow holds a tale untold,
Cradled close, like jewels of gold.

A flicker of light, the softest sigh,
In the dark, secrets dare to fly.
With every breath, the night unfolds,
Revealing wonders, brave and bold.

The moon, a guardian of the still,
Watches over the world at will.
In whispered tones, the night confides,
Hiding truths where magic bides.

In this dance of mist and night,
Hearts entwined in fleeting light.
Embrace the echoes, hear their call,
For in the mist, we find it all.

The Luminance of Shifting Shadows

As daylight fades and shadows weave,
A tapestry of night, believe.
Fleeting forms in sleek display,
Dancing softly, drift away.

In the luminescent glow of stars,
Every twinkle soothes our scars.
Life's mysteries twirl in delight,
Painting tales in the soft twilight.

Flickers of laughter, sighs and tears,
Echo across the span of years.
The dance of shadows, bold and free,
Whispers secrets of you and me.

When dusk embraces, shadows play,
Life unfolds in shades of gray.
Enchantments swirl with every breath,
In laughter's glow, transcending death.

Thus, hold the light in every shade,
For in the depths, the magic's laid.
In shifting shadows, we reside,
Embrace the dance, let love abide.

Dreamweaver's Veil

In the realm where dreams take flight,
A tapestry spun from silver light.
The Dreamweaver beckons, soft and sly,
Creating worlds where spirits fly.

Through the veil of twilight's gleam,
Whispers echo of a forgotten dream.
Each sigh carries a wish unmade,
Painting paths where shadows played.

Stars whisper secrets in the deep,
Cradling thoughts that gently creep.
With tender care, the night unfolds,
Revealing treasures yet untold.

Embrace the magic, let it in,
Where dreams delight and twilight begins.
With every heartbeat, time stands still,
In the fabric of dreams, we find our will.

So close your eyes and drift away,
Within the veil where wishes sway.
For in this world of soft embrace,
Lies the beauty of our grace.

Dreaming in the Enchanted Twilight

In twilight's hush, our dreams take flight,
Beneath the stars, in velvet night.
Whispers dance on a gentle breeze,
Magic stirs among the trees.

With moonlit paths and shadows deep,
Where ancient secrets softly creep.
A world unseen, yet felt so near,
In every sigh, we sense the clear.

The magic hums like a sweet refrain,
A symphony of joy and pain.
While fireflies weave their golden thread,
Illuminating the dreams we've bred.

So close your eyes, let wonders bloom,
In dreams of twilight, dispel the gloom.
For every heart that dares to dream,
Finds solace in the starlit beam.

Awake, dear soul, to morning's glow,
With tales of twilight in tow.
Embrace the day with a gentle sigh,
For life's enchanted, and so are we.

Secrets of the Glistening Glade

In glistening glades where shadows play,
Secrets hide by night and day.
Beneath the boughs of ancient trees,
Echoes linger in the breeze.

The brook murmurs tales of old,
Of knights and quests, of treasures bold.
Each leaf that rustles tells a truth,
A whisper of lost, forgotten youth.

Mossy stones guard the aged lore,
Of magic spells, of mythic war.
When twilight falls, the faeries roam,
To weave enchantments, far from home.

Wander not with hasty feet,
In this realm where past and present meet.
For every step reveals a clue,
To long-lost dreams and spirits true.

So linger long, let worries fade,
Find comfort in this secret glade.
For here, the heart shall always soar,
In nature's arms, forevermore.

Mists of the Celestial Meadow

In meadows where the mists arise,
Beneath the watchful, starlit skies.
Dreams weave into the morning light,
A tapestry of pure delight.

Each dew-kissed petal, soft and bright,
Cradles whispers of the night.
The air is thick with magic's breath,
Where dreams are born, and shadows rest.

With every step, enchantments grow,
In celestial realms, the spirits flow.
A lullaby of nature sings,
As dawn unfolds her golden wings.

Here in the hush, time ceases still,
With every pulse, an ancient thrill.
For in this place, so wild and free,
All souls converge in harmony.

So seek this meadow, lost yet found,
Where dreams and silence wrap around.
In the mists, our hearts take flight,
In the dance of day and night.

Whispered Tales of the Dappled Dawn

In dawning light where shadows fade,
Whispered tales are gently made.
The sun spills warmth on the waking land,
With every ray, a guiding hand.

Upon the hills, the fog recedes,
Revealing life in vibrant beads.
Birdsong trills through the bending boughs,
A symphony of nature's vows.

Through dappled paths, the dreams unfold,
Of fabled heroes brave and bold.
Each step we take, a story spun,
In morning's grasp, new hopes begun.

The world awakens from its rest,
With every heart a tender quest.
So take my hand, let's wander far,
In search of dreams, beneath the star.

For in the dawn, all things align,
With whispered tales and destiny's sign.
In the light of day, we'll still embrace,
The magic woven in every place.

Dream Castles in the Hazy Ether

In the air where shadows play,
Drift on dreams that sail away.
Clouds like whispers softly weave,
Crafting tales we dare believe.

Each tower built of starlit sighs,
Glittering under velvet skies.
Winds that carry secrets bold,
Stories of the brave, the old.

Fantastical, the walls that gleam,
Rubies spark in moonlit beam.
Here in realms not bound by time,
Heartstrings dance in joyous rhyme.

Floating high, where hopes ignite,
Every star a guiding light.
In this place, let spirits soar,
Chasing dreams forevermore.

So wander in this endless maze,
Of golden nights and silver days.
Dream castles call, with open gates,
To realms where every heart awaits.

Celestial Traces Beneath the Trees

Beneath the boughs where whispers dwell,
Ancient secrets start to swell.
Stars descend and kiss the ground,
In this haven, magic's found.

Footsteps light on mossy beds,
Where the silver brooklet spreads.
Luminous trails where fairies dance,
In the twilight's soft romance.

Branches weave a tapestry,
Nature's art, it's plain to see.
Catch the glimmers through the leaves,
In this space, the heart believes.

Echoes of a world so grand,
Whispers from a distant land.
Beneath the trees, let spirits rise,
With every gaze towards the skies.

So sit in silence, hear the song,
The universe has waited long.
In this grove where dreams unfold,
Celestial traces softly told.

The Underglow of Mystical Realms

In the dusk where shadows blend,
Secrets of the night descend.
Glimmers twinkle in the dark,
Echoes of a distant spark.

Threads of light on woven ground,
In this realm, lost souls are found.
Each corner hides a tale untold,
Where ancient magic, bright and bold.

Crickets sing a lullaby,
Beneath the watchful, winking sky.
In every breath, a story lingers,
Woven tight with fate's own fingers.

Feel the pulse of life's embrace,
In this mystical, sacred space.
Here, the echoes softly roam,
Whispers of a forgotten home.

So, wander forth where magic calls,
In the underglow of ancient halls.
For the realms that dance with chance,
Invite you in, in vibrant trance.

Twilight Whispers Among the Thistles

As the sun dips low in sighs,
Twilight whispers, sweet goodbyes.
Among the thistles, shadows sway,
In the dusk, dreams find their way.

Breezes hum a soothing tune,
Tickling hearts in the soft cocoon.
Fireflies flicker, stars ignite,
Guiding souls through gentle night.

Each petal brushed by fading light,
Sways to melodies of night.
In the quiet, secrets blend,
A dance of time that knows no end.

Whispers soft, like spun-out lace,
In this garden, find your place.
Let your worries drift away,
In the twilight's warm embrace.

So linger long, and breathe it in,
Where the magic waits within.
Among the thistles, softly sway,
As the night unveils the day.

Intriguing Shadows Beneath the Ancient Canopy

In the woods where whispers dwell,
Shadows dance, a mystic spell.
Ancient trees with secrets hold,
Stories of the brave and bold.

Mist rises soft from earth to sky,
Where creatures creep and fairies fly.
Roots entwined in silent grace,
Nature hides in this sacred space.

A rustle in the ferns nearby,
Echoes of a forgotten sigh.
The moon peeks through the leafed embrace,
Illuminating the hidden place.

Beneath the boughs, time drifts away,
History lingers, twilight's play.
Softly calling on the breeze,
Life in shadows, nature's tease.

Each footstep cradles ancient lore,
Yet all is whispered, nevermore.
In twilight's hush, secrets confide,
The ancient canopy, a guardian wide.

The Soft Serenade of Delicate Phantoms

In moonlit glades where phantoms sing,
A gentle tune on soft winds wing.
Delicate whispers in the trees,
Carried far on twilight's breeze.

Luminous shades in evening's glow,
Dance to rhythms only they know.
Twinkling stardust, a silken thread,
Woven tales of those long dead.

Gossamer dreams take playful flight,
Swaying gently in the night.
Echoes of laughter, sweet and clear,
Phantoms waltz without a fear.

With every note, weaves a spell,
Enchantment cast like a silver bell.
Through the forest, their voices roam,
Soft serenades that feel like home.

Underneath the velvet sky,
Time stands still; we cannot lie.
These specters whisper, tender and bright,
The path to dreams, in the soft night.

Incandescent Hues in the Heart of Night

When shadows fall, a canvas blooms,
Incandescent shades dispel the glooms.
Deep indigos and vibrant golds,
Color the night with stories bold.

Stars awaken, a shimmering tide,
Rippling across the moonlit side.
Each glittering gem, a wish whispered,
In the cosmic dance, so softly mirrored.

Whispers of dawn brush the horizon,
As night's embrace feels like a siren.
Colors swirling, weaving dreams bright,
A masterpiece painted in the night.

In this realm where vision drifts,
Magic stirs and the heart lifts.
Incandescent hues unite the stunned,
In shadows deep, our worries shunned.

With every glance, a veil is torn,
Bearing hope through the night reborn.
In the heart of dark, there's a spark,
Incandescent hues, igniting the dark.

Flickering Thoughts in the Cosmic Veil

Beneath the sweep of endless skies,
Flickering thoughts like fireflies rise.
They dart and dance in swirling glow,
In the cosmic veil, where wonders flow.

Each twinkle holds a dream untold,
A secret light wrapped in the cold.
Moments captured, then released,
Whispers of the universe, increased.

In this dreamscape, time is a sea,
Swirling gently, forever free.
The mind drifts where the stars conspire,
To ignite the soul with a spark of fire.

Thoughts like comets blaze and wane,
Leaving traces of joy and pain.
Through the vastness, our stories meld,
In flickering thoughts, our paths upheld.

In the stillness where silence sings,
Resonates the joy that dreaming brings.
Through the cosmos, hearts prevail,
Flickering thoughts in the cosmic veil.

Moonlit Dances in the Faeries' Embrace

Under the glow of a silver moon,
Faeries twirl in a soft, sweet tune.
They weave through the shadows, light as mist,
In a world where the dreamers' hearts persist.

Petals unfurl beneath the stars,
Whispers of magic from afar.
Their laughter flickers like candlelight,
Guiding the lost through the velvet night.

Glimmering wings like sparkling dew,
Embrace the secrets known to few.
Frolic and play in the ancient glade,
Where hopes are nurtured and never fade.

With every step, the night comes alive,
In the dance where only dreamers strive.
The moonlight bathes all in wonderous hues,
Awakening stories that time will not lose.

So join the faeries in their bright flights,
Where every heart sings of fleeting sights.
In the embrace of this mystical space,
We find ourselves in the faeries' grace.

Luminescent Trails in the Realm of Dreams

In the realm where day meets the night,
Glow the trails of dreams, soft and bright.
Follow them gently, let your heart soar,
Into the depths of the mind's open door.

With each step forward, a vision unfolds,
Stories of silver, of treasures untold.
Caught in the whispers of dusk's tender care,
Woven in shadows that dance in the air.

Shapes twist and shimmer in colors so bold,
Guided by starlight, a sight to behold.
Fables and fantasies start to materialize,
As time unwinds in a glittering guise.

Floating on currents of vibrant delight,
Chasing the echoes that shimmer at night.
Every heartbeat leads to a dreamer's embrace,
In the world where all thoughts find their place.

So wander through dreams, let your spirit glide,
In luminescent trails, let magic reside.
For in this realm, the impossible gleams,
And life unfolds in a tapestry of dreams.

Cascading Whispers on the Edge of Reality

On the brink where the real and unreal dance,
Cascading whispers beckon, a fleeting chance.
Ethereal moments weave stories anew,
Life's fragile thread binds the me and you.

A flicker of light in the shadows below,
Hints of existence in the moon's mellow glow.
Listen intently, let your heart speak,
In the silence, a truth that we seek.

Suspended between what is dream and what's true,
The world sways gently in shades of blue.
Every soft murmur steals breaths from the air,
Carried on currents of magic laid bare.

As night deepens, the whispers grow clear,
Revealing the mysteries we hold most dear.
Embrace the unknown, let your spirit roam,
Between the realms, you will find your home.

For on the edge of reality's plea,
We discover the beauty of what is to be.
In cascading whispers, we dance with the night,
Creating our dreams in the warmth of twilight.

The Allure of Tenuous Fantasies at Dusk

As the sun dips low and the shadows grow long,
Tenuous fantasies sing a sweet song.
Elusive like whispers that tickle the air,
They beckon us softly, igniting our care.

Colors of twilight paint skies in deep gold,
Stories of dreams in soft tones unfold.
Each flicker of thought dances close to the heart,
Embracing the magic as night bids us start.

The allure of wishes wrapped in a sigh,
Hopes drift like clouds in the gentle sky.
With every heartbeat, the dusk reveals,
The treasures of life and the joy it yields.

In the quiet of evening, all worries are shed,
Opening the door to worlds in our head.
A tapestry woven with threads like gossamer,
As the dreams take flight, our spirits concur.

So linger a moment, let fantasies bloom,
In the dusk's tender glow, let the night resume.
For in every heartbeat, we find our own way,
Through tenuous journeys where dreamers will stay.

Enchanted Mist on the Sylvan Path

In twilight's glow, the mist unveils,
A hidden world where magic sails.
With emerald leaves and whispers sweet,
The sylvan path beneath my feet.

Each step I take, the fairies dance,
In shades of light, they weave a trance.
The gentle breeze, it calls my name,
A realm where wonders spark the flame.

The silver brook, it laughs and sings,
As nature plays with secret things.
Through bramble thick and shadows deep,
In this enchanted dream, I leap.

The ancient trees, they guard the night,
With stories old and wisdom bright.
I breathe the magic, feel it bloom,
In every corner, life finds room.

So here I roam, in mist, I'm lost,
In sylvan realms, I pay the cost.
For every glance, a charm I draw,
In this enchanted haven's awe.

Shrouded Secrets of the Mystical Dell

In the mystical dell, where shadows blend,
The secrets of ages, they softly send.
Old stones whisper with tales untold,
Of creatures curious, brave, and bold.

The willow weeps with silver tears,
A guardian of forgotten years.
Its branches sway in whispered sighs,
As magic unfolds beneath the skies.

Through tangled roots, the spirits hum,
In melodies soft, like a distant drum.
The air is thick with mystery,
A place where fate spins history.

The flowers bloom in vibrant hues,
Each petal cradles ancient clues.
In this dell, where dreams collide,
I watch the worlds of magic bide.

With every breath, I feel the pull,
Of tales unspoken, wondrous, full.
I wander deeper, night unfolds,
In twilight's hand, the story holds.

Flickering Light Beneath the Canopy

Beneath the canopy, where shadows play,
Flickering lights drive the darkness away.
With fireflies dancing, like stars in flight,
They weave a tapestry of pure delight.

The nightingale sings her lilting song,
In this realm, where dreams belong.
Each note a spark, igniting the air,
A symphony of magic, raw and rare.

Branches arch like arms of old,
Embracing tales of the brave and bold.
I close my eyes and feel the grace,
Of every shadow, every place.

Moonlight glimmers on emerald leaves,
In this quiet world, my heart believes.
With every flicker, stories glow,
Of ancient paths and the tales they know.

As night gives way to dawn's embrace,
I find my peace in this sacred space.
With flickering lights as my guide,
Beneath the canopy, I abide.

Veiled Whispers of the Eldergrove

In the eldergrove, where shadows breathe,
Veiled whispers float like threads to weave.
Old oaks stand guard with solemn grace,
Their branches hold a sacred space.

The grasses sway in silken hush,
As secrets linger in every crush.
Invisible hands press upon my heart,
In the veil of night, worlds drift apart.

Moss carpets soft the forest floor,
While chants of nature begin to pour.
The air is thick with stories spun,
Of ancient battles lost and won.

As I wander through this mystic lore,
The elder trees beckon me to explore.
With every step, I dive profound,
In hidden realms where dreams abound.

So let me linger, hear their call,
In this eldergrove where spirits fall.
Veiled whispers guide my way anew,
As night unfolds its cloak of dew.

Starlit Auras on Gentle Swells

The moonlight dances on the sea,
Whispers of magic ride the breeze.
Each wave a secret, soft and free,
Underneath the starlit trees.

A symphony of night unfolds,
Golden dreams woven in the tide.
Stories of wonders gently told,
As the world in wonder hides.

Glimmers of hope in the dark,
Echoes of laughter, sweet and pure.
With every pulse, the night leaves a mark,
In the heart where dreams endure.

Silver shimmers on the crest,
Guiding souls through azure light.
A tranquil haven, simply blessed,
Enfolded in the still of night.

As starlit auras softly gleam,
So the ocean cradles its swell.
In every drop, a vibrant dream,
In every whisper, a tale to tell.

Fables Whispered Through the Wisps

In the heart of the whispering wood,
Fables dance at the breath of dawn.
Every tree knows the stories good,
As shadows stretch and yawn.

Through the mist, an old tale flows,
Spun by the breeze, soft and light.
With every rustling leaf that glows,
Magic stirs in the silent night.

Wandering spirits weave their sounds,
Echoes of laughter, old and wise.
In every corner, wonder abounds,
Bright as the morning skies.

In twilight's embrace, dreams ignite,
Colors paint the fading air.
Each fable danced in soft twilight,
Is a treasure beyond compare.

So listen close to the gentle sighs,
Of the forest, alive and true.
For in the whispers, the magic lies,
Awaiting to find you.

Silvery Laughter Amongst Elysian Shadows

With every sunset, laughter stirs,
Amongst the shadows, soft and bright.
A symphony of giggles occurs,
Echoing through the gentle night.

In the realm where dreams entwine,
Elysian whispers fill the air.
Each sigh is sweet, like aged wine,
A moment lost, and yet so rare.

As stars awaken, secrets bloom,
Laughter dances in hushed tones.
Filling the heart, dispelling gloom,
In a paradise of twilight stones.

Beneath the sky's velvet embrace,
Shadows twirl in a joyous spree.
The world is wrapped in a tender grace,
As twinkling stars weave a melody.

So here within this enchanted glade,
Let silvery laughter roam free.
For in the shadows, magic is made,
And the night holds its own decree.

Citadels of Magic in Ethereal Clouds

Above the world, where whispers soar,
Citadels rise from misty dreams.
Crafted in light forevermore,
Flowing on invisible beams.

These towers of wonder kiss the skies,
Every stair holds spells and charms.
In clouds that crash like sweet surprise,
The heart of magic softly warms.

Beneath the glow of celestial light,
Mysteries linger, softly spun.
In the embrace of endless night,
Weaving tales that will not be done.

Glimmers of hope in each hidden nook,
Stardust dances on the air.
In every turn, an open book,
With secrets that the brave may share.

So step into this realm divine,
Where ethereal clouds invite you near.
Citadels of magic intertwine,
In every heartbeat, pure and clear.

Whispers of the Enchanted Mist

In the twilight glow, secrets weave,
Softly spoken, hearts believe.
Misty veils that dance and sway,
Carry dreams that drift away.

Silent echoes in the night,
Crickets sing, a soft delight.
Shadows flicker, magic calls,
Enchanted whispers line the walls.

Through the fog, a pathway glows,
Where the wild, sweet breezes blow.
Underneath the ancient trees,
Nature breathes with gentle ease.

Fairy lights in laughter twirl,
A hidden world begins to swirl.
Lost in tales of long ago,
The mist reveals what few can know.

So linger long beneath the shade,
In realms where dreams and fears invade.
For in the mist, our stories blend,
An endless journey, without end.

Shadows Dancing on Ethereal Greens

Beneath the boughs where shadows play,
In whispers soft, they weave their way.
The ferns sway gentle, spirits sing,
A lullaby the forest brings.

Dappled light through leaves does gleam,
Colorful echoes of a dream.
Unseen dancers twirl and sway,
Painting love in shades of day.

With every breath, the magic stirs,
In rustling leaves, the joy occurs.
Bright butterflies in the warm, sunbeam,
Spread color like a painter's theme.

The mossy floor, a velvet bed,
Where fairy tales are softly read.
Listen close, the secrets gleam,
In every sigh, a hidden dream.

So linger in this sacred space,
Where shadows weave with tender grace.
Embrace the dance, the earth's delight,
In every heartbeat, purest light.

Secrets Woven in Gossamer Air

In twilight's weave, the whispers spin,
Threads of magic gently begin.
Gossamer strands in the evening light,
Hold the secrets of the night.

Moonbeams kiss the dreams awake,
Softly swirling, gentle flake.
In the hush, the stories told,
Of love and loss, of brave and bold.

The air is thick with longing sighs,
Echoes of laughter, gentle cries.
Each breeze carries a tale anew,
In woven whispers, old and true.

Through wooded paths, the shadows glide,
In leafy cloisters, whispers bide.
Follow where the heartbeats roam,
In gossamer dreams, you'll find your home.

From every glade, the murmurs rise,
Bright memories 'neath starlit skies.
Secrets shared in the quiet air,
With every breath, they linger there.

Mirage of Hallowed Whispers

In the stillness of the dawn,
Hallowed whispers stretch and yawn.
Like a mist that rises slow,
Giving life to all we know.

Each soft echo holds a truth,
Of lost time and fleeting youth.
With every sigh, we chase the past,
In mirage dreams, shadows cast.

The golden rays of sunlight dance,
Inviting all to take a chance.
Where dreams and reality blend,
At the dawn, the worlds transcend.

So heed the call of morning light,
Embrace the magic, take to flight.
For in the whispers, tales reside,
With every breath, the heart's confide.

A mirage forms in gentle air,
Promising wonders everywhere.
So linger soft, let hopes unfurl,
Within these whispers, find your world.

Enchanted Landscapes on the Edge of Dreams

Whispers dance upon the breeze,
Beneath the twilight's soft embrace.
Mountains wear their misty crowns,
While rivers weave a timeless lace.

Glimmers of the fading light,
Paint the forest's emerald hue.
Ancient trees stand tall and wise,
Guardians of the night anew.

Secrets whispered 'neath the stars,
In shadows where the fairies play.
Moonbeams trace a silver path,
Leading wanderers astray.

In this realm where dreams take flight,
Magic folds and bends the night.
Every sigh and tender glance,
Invites the heart to join the dance.

As dawn awakens with a sigh,
The golden sun begins to rise.
Yet still, the echoes of the night,
Lurk softly in the morning skies.

Visceral Echoes Along Eldritch Paths

Through tangled woods, the shadows creep,
Whispers echo, secrets keep.
Branches twist in eerie forms,
Nature's heart, a storm that warms.

Footsteps lead to realms unseen,
Where the veil of night feels keen.
Runes inscribed on ancient stone,
Tell of tales long overgrown.

A howl breaks the fragile air,
Beasts unseen, a lurking stare.
Misty fog, a cloak of dread,
Fills the night with thoughts unsaid.

Through veils of dusk, a flicker glows,
Guiding hearts where danger flows.
In the dark, a truth ignites,
Echoing through endless nights.

Upon the path, the brave must tread,
Where past and future both are wed.
Each footstep holds a twisted tale,
Of echoes lost, where spirits wail.

Remnants of Starlight in Shaded Glens

In valleys deep where shadows reign,
The light retreats, yet leaves its stain.
Softly glows the evening mist,
Kisses dreams that still persist.

Beneath the boughs where silence sleeps,
Twinkling stars their vigil keeps.
Each glimmer a forgotten wish,
Lingering like a tender kiss.

The winds weave tales of yesteryears,
Carrying laughter, love, and tears.
Rustling leaves in quiet reverie,
Whisper secrets of destiny.

In this glen where shadows fall,
Ghosts of time still softly call.
A symphony of dreams takes flight,
As remnants glow in silver light.

Awake, the heart shall take its stand,
Embrace the beauty of this land.
For in the still, the past remains,
A dance of starlight in our veins.

Mystical Murmurs Through the Verdant Fold

Nestled deep in emerald sways,
The forest hums in secret ways.
A tapestry of dreams unfold,
In paths where ancient legends told.

Misted trails invite the bold,
To venture where the fables mold.
Parfumed blooms in twilight's grace,
Drape the earth in soft embrace.

Crickets sing their twilight tune,
Beneath the watchful, silver moon.
Each note a promise, every sound,
A pulse of magic all around.

In tender glades, the fae reside,
With whispered charms to turn the tide.
They invite the weary heart to dance,
In the twilight's fleeting glance.

Within this fold, where time stands still,
Dreamers seek what hearts fulfill.
So linger here, let worries cease,
And find your path to inner peace.

Secrets of the Sylvan Realm at Dawn

The whisper of leaves in the morning light,
Where shadows dance with the fading night.
Sky painted gold, a soft morning hue,
Beneath emerald canopies, secrets ensue.

Moss carpets the ground, a silken green,
In every glade, a whispered dream.
Creatures awaken, the world feels alive,
In the Sylvan realm, the heart starts to thrive.

The brook's gentle babble, a melodic flow,
Carries the tales of the seeds that we sow.
Sunbeams flutter like fairies on wings,
In this enchanted realm, pure magic clings.

Laughter of sprites, a sound so rare,
Chasing the dew with delicate flair.
Nature's symphony, at dawn's soft kiss,
Holds within it all the world's bliss.

A fleeting moment, soon to depart,
Yet etched forever deep in the heart.
The dawn unfolds, the secret it hides,
In the Sylvan realm, where wonder abides.

Sighs of Whimsy in the Flickering Air

In twilight's glow, where shadows play,
Whispers of whimsy come out to sway.
Breeze like a secret, stirring the leaves,
In the flickering air, the heart believes.

Dancing fireflies weave through the night,
Their glow a spark, a soft delight.
Invisible threads of dreams interlace,
In the dusk's embrace, we find our place.

The sigh of a moonbeam, a gentle caress,
Wrapping the world in a silvery dress.
Each star a wink, each cloud a sigh,
Through whimsy's breath, we learn to fly.

Echoes of laughter linger so sweet,
In cobblestone paths where shadows meet.
A tapestry woven with the shade of night,
In fleeting moments, our spirits take flight.

With every breeze, a story unfolds,
In whispers of magic that never grows old.
In the flickering air, where dreams do twirl,
Sighs of whimsy breathe life to the world.

Melodies of the Heart Beneath Floating Haze

In the morning mist, all senses awake,
The world draped in grey, a delicate flake.
Each heartbeat echoes through shrouded space,
Melodies waltz in this tranquil place.

Veils of fog dance with a spectral grace,
Hiding the edges of time and pace.
Songs of the ancients whisper so low,
In the floating haze, where dreams freely flow.

Rays of the sun pierce the cool morning air,
Illuminating secrets we long to share.
With notes that flutter like leaves from a tree,
In this misty haven, we learn to be free.

Harmony sings in the rustling grass,
As moments dissolve like the dew in the mass.
Beneath the haze, our hearts gently sway,
To the rhythm of life, come what may.

As the haze lifts, clarity reigns,
In the melodies born from the heart's strains.
With every note, a bond we create,
In the floating haze, we celebrate fate.

The Allure of Twilight's Gentle Caress

As day turns to night, in a soft embrace,
Twilight drapes the world in a silken lace.
Stars peek shyly, one by one,
In the golden aftermath of the setting sun.

A hush blankets valleys, a soothing balm,
Nature sprawls in the twilight's calm.
Whispers of futures and dreams yet to come,
In this radiant hour, our hearts beat as one.

The sky blushes pink, with hints of gold,
Stories of ages in silence unfold.
Promises linger like dew on the grass,
In twilight's allure, we gently amass.

Fireflies emerge in a gentle ballet,
Painting the dusk with their luminous play.
Each flicker a promise, each dance a song,
In twilight's embrace, where we all belong.

As night takes its throne, the world feels new,
In the allure of twilight, everything's true.
We gather the stars, weaving dreams that impress,
In the gentle caress of this soft, sweet success.

Celestial Haze Over Faery Fields

In twilight's glow where shadows play,
The faery lights begin to sway.
Whispers of magic fill the air,
A realm of wonder, bright and rare.

Beneath the stars, the flowers gleam,
In every petal, a secret dream.
The breeze carries tales of old,
Of daring hearts and treasures bold.

A silver moon, a watchful eye,
Guides the lost on nights gone by.
With laughter echoing through the trees,
Soft murmurs float upon the breeze.

Among the glades, in tranquil peace,
Where time endures and sorrows cease.
The faeries twirl in silver light,
Crafting magic from the night.

In celestial haze, their dances weave,
A tapestry of dreams, believe.
With every heartbeat, dreams take flight,
In faery fields, where souls unite.

Covert Trails of Shimmering Dreams

Underneath a sky of stars,
The dreamers wander, near and far.
On hidden paths, where wishes glide,
In realms where secret hopes abide.

With every step, the starlight glows,
Illuminating where magic flows.
Soft glimmers dance upon the stone,
In covert trails, the dreams are sown.

Moonlit streams and shadowed glades,
In whispered tales, the night invades.
Enchanted woodlands softly hum,
To calls of faery, gently come.

In silver mists, where shadows meet,
The heart begins to find its beat.
With every secret softly spun,
In shimmering dreams, our lives are won.

A world awash in whispered grace,
Inviting all to join the chase.
In every heart, a spark ignites,
On covert trails, in endless flights.

Dance of the Faded Fae

In twilight's grasp where silence clings,
The faded fae share tender flings.
Once vibrant wings, now soft and light,
In gentle motions, they take flight.

With every twirl, they weave a spell,
In echoes soft that time won't quell.
A dance of joy, of memories lost,
In sinuous steps, they count the cost.

Their laughter mingles with the breeze,
A tune that soothes, a heart to please.
In dreary days of fading light,
Their spirits rise, defying night.

Among the glimmers, they intertwine,
In silken threads of fate, divine.
Their faded hues, a palette bright,
Shimmering softly in the night.

Waltzing on through the moonlit shade,
In hushed reveries, dreams are laid.
They gather joy from every tear,
In dance of the faded, love draws near.

Labyrinth of the Enchanted Thicket

In thickets deep where shadows creep,
A labyrinth waits, its secrets keep.
Each twist and turn a mystery,
In every path, a tapestry.

Amidst the leaves, the faeries play,
Guiding wanderers on their way.
With pixie dust and laughter light,
They lead the lost from dark to bright.

A gentle mist cloaks every stone,
While whispers round, in softest tone.
Through tangled roots, in silence tread,
Where every heart is lightly led.

Within the maze, the wonders bloom,
Invoking joy, dispelling gloom.
In every corner, creatures cheer,
An enchanted world that draws you near.

So step inside, with dreams in hand,
As fate unfolds, a magic land.
In labyrinth's heart, your spirit glows,
In enchanted thicket, love bestows.

Glimmers of Hope in the Veil of Night

In the dark where shadows creep,
A twinkle stirs, secrets to keep.
Stars whisper dreams in silver light,
Guiding lost souls through the night.

Beneath the boughs of ancient trees,
A gentle sigh rides on the breeze.
Hope flickers in the hearts of the brave,
As dawn awakens from its cave.

In every corner, a story waits,
Of magical lands and whispered fates.
Faint echoes dance on twilight's seam,
Binding reality to a dream.

With every breath, the silence breaks,
Awakening wonders that twilight makes.
For in the veil, a promise lies,
A glimmering truth beneath the skies.

So walk with courage, and do not fear,
For hope's sweet song is always near.
Through shadows deep, let your spirit soar,
Glimmers of hope forever more.

Threads of Light in a Misty Union

In the fog where colors blend,
Threads of light begin to send.
A tapestry woven of dreams and sighs,
Binding together the earth and skies.

With each strand, a tale unfurls,
Of distant lands and whispering pearls.
In hidden glens, magic takes flight,
Fleeting moments wrapped in night.

Stars weave patterns in the gloom,
As shadows dance, dispelling doom.
A melody lingers in the air,
A song of longing, soft and rare.

Through the mist, bright visions float,
Each one a wish, a hopeful note.
In every heart, a spark ignites,
Threads of light in misty nights.

So follow the glow where the path may lead,
For in each step, the soul is freed.
In this union of twilight's grace,
Find love and courage in every place.

The Breath of Twilight on Faery Wings

As day gives way to veils of dusk,
Faeries dance with a fragrant musk.
Their laughter sparkles, a silvery ring,
On the breath of twilight, the night takes wing.

In whispered dreams and silent charms,
They weave enchantments, stirring hearts' warms.
A gentle caress in the twilight air,
A sprinkle of magic beyond compare.

With every flutter, shadows fade,
As starlit skies in secrets cascade.
In the hush of night, they softly sing,
Of ancient tales on faery wings.

So listen closely, and you may find,
The breath of twilight, gentle and kind.
It wraps around like a lover's embrace,
Leading us softly to that hidden place.

For in the night, when dreams take flight,
The faeries bring wonder and delight.
Through every heartbeat, every sting,
Feel the magic on faery wings.

Dappled Daydreams in the Moonlit Hollow

In a hollow where shadows play,
Moonlight drapes the night in gray.
Dappled dreams twine through the trees,
Carried aloft by the softest breeze.

Whispers linger in the cool air,
Echoes of laughter, secrets laid bare.
In twilight's grasp, enchantments gleam,
As starlit visions weave a seam.

Crickets serenade with notes so sweet,
While fireflies flit in a rhythmic beat.
Each pulse of light tells a story anew,
Of worlds unseen, of skies so blue.

In this place where magic dwells,
A precious peace within us swells.
Close your eyes, let the laughter flow,
In the moonlit hollow, let dreams bestow.

For here in the quiet, hearts entwine,
Dappled daydreams, a love divine.
With every breath, let your spirit roam,
In the moonlit hollow, you are home.

The Enigma of Faded Echoes at Sundown

Whispers linger where shadows play,
In twilight hues, the light will sway.
Memories dance on a golden thread,
As dusk enfolds the world in red.

Soft murmurs rise from the ancient wood,
Elden secrets in silence stood.
Each rustle speaks of times long past,
Echoes fade but their truths hold fast.

The sun dips low, the sky ignites,
Flames of orange, a couplet of sights.
Among the tales woven with care,
Each fading echo, a fragrant air.

In this moment, all seems to blend,
The past and present without an end.
The heart, it listens, the soul, it yearns,
For the echoes of time, as the twilight burns.

Clarity cloaked in the night so deep,
Within its grasp, the shadows keep.
At day's farewell, the secrets swell,
As magic weaves its mystic spell.

Gossamer Touches of Forgotten Lore

Amidst the dusk where dreams are spun,
Soft glimmers trace what's lost, undone.
The air is thick with stories told,
In whispers soft, their threads unfold.

Gossamer strands of ancient fate,
Penning tales that time won't abate.
Each shimmer, a note in a melody,
A love letter written in epiphany.

Through thickets where the wild leaves sway,
Forgotten tomes linger, and softly play.
Their voices weave between the trees,
Carried forth on the gentle breeze.

In twilight's embrace, the lore takes flight,
Reaching for stars, igniting the night.
In the fabric of dusk, magic unfurls,
Whispers of ancient, forgotten worlds.

As shadows lengthen with each passing hour,
The echoes of lore blossom like a flower.
With delicate grace, the tales unfurl,
In gossamer touches, they dance and twirl.

Mirage-Soft Flesh in Glistening Ferns

In the glade where the ferns caress,
Soft whispers hide in nature's dress.
Mirages glisten, bending the light,
Evoking dreams that waltz in flight.

With tender grace, the shadows weave,
A tapestry of magic we believe.
Every leaf tells a story unchained,
In glistening veils, enchantments sustained.

Underneath the boughs, the secret lies,
A dance of truth in the midnight cries.
Fleeting spirits pulse with the breeze,
In the softest flesh of glistening leaves.

With every rustle, a beckoning call,
Whispered tales in the twilight's sprawl.
Each step forward, the earth will sing,
Of mirage-soft flesh and the joy it brings.

Where reality blurs and dreams entwine,
In ferns' embrace, our spirits align.
In the whispering dusk, we find our grace,
As mirage-joy fills the sacred space.

A Reverie Entwined With Nature's Breath

Beneath the sky where the wildflowers bloom,
Nature whispers, dispelling the gloom.
In this reverie, dreams take flight,
Entwined with the breath of soft twilight.

Through meadows kissed by the evening air,
The heart finds solace, a quiet prayer.
Each petal, a promise, each leaf, a vow,
A symphony played by the dusk somehow.

Gentle shadows play on the grassy plain,
A serenade sung in a sweet refrain.
The night unfolds with its tender grace,
Wrapping the world in a warm embrace.

Lost in the rhythm of nature's song,
A dance of harmony where we belong.
In softest whispers, the night will weave,
A tale of reverie, a heart to relieve.

So breathe in deeply, let worries cease,
In twilight's arms, embrace the peace.
For in this moment, hearts will confess,
A reverie entwined with nature's breath.

Enigma of the Wandering Vapors

In twilight's glow, the shadows creep,
The vapors swirl, their secrets keep.
With whispered tales of ages past,
They drift like dreams, both slow and fast.

Beneath the moon's soft silver sheen,
The night unveils what lurks unseen.
Ghostly forms in quiet dance,
In every glimmer, there's a chance.

Through twisted woods where echoes sigh,
The vapors float, they never die.
They weave a web of mystic sight,
A tapestry of dark and light.

Each wisp a story, long forgotten,
In nature's breath, the lost is begotten.
With every step, a shiver chills,
As magic lingers, time stands still.

So roam the paths where secrets lie,
Embrace the night, the endless sky.
For in the dance of vapors' flight,
You'll find the truth within the night.

Serendipity on Silvery Breezes

Upon the winds where laughter plays,
Serendipity in gentle sways.
The whispers of the trees confide,
In breezes soft, hope not to hide.

Each note a promise, sweetly spun,
In silver light, new dreams begun.
With every rustle, joy ignites,
A symphony of pure delights.

Beneath the stars, the world unfolds,
In moments captured, life beholds.
A gentle nudge, a lucky chance,
As hearts entwine in nature's dance.

With open hearts, we drift along,
As serendipity sings its song.
In every breeze, a tale to tell,
A magic woven, cast a spell.

So linger on this path so rare,
Embrace the joy that lingers there.
For in the twist of fate's embrace,
You'll find your wonder, your true place.

Haunting Melodies in Nature's Cloak

With twilight draped in nature's cloak,
A melody, the woods evoke.
In every rustling leaf and sigh,
A haunting tune that sweeps the sky.

The wind weaves tales of long ago,
In whispers soft, a gentle flow.
Each note a phantom of the past,
In echoes deep, the shadows cast.

The stars above begin to gleam,
As night ignites a dusky dream.
The world around starts to conspire,
With sounds that weave and hearts that fire.

From gnarled roots to branches wide,
The haunting tones no soul can hide.
In twilight's arms, we find our way,
To melodies that softly sway.

So let the music guide your feet,
In nature's arms, your heart will meet.
For in each haunting, lovely tune,
A tapestry of night and moon.

Dance of the Spirits on Velvet Fields

In velvet fields where shadows lay,
The spirits rise in soft ballet.
With every twirl, the grasses sway,
And nightingale sang 'til break of day.

From dawn to dusk, they glide and weave,
In whispers shared, the air they cleave.
The fragrant blooms bow down in grace,
As time dissolves within their trace.

A waltz of laughter, a hush of thought,
In every note, a lesson sought.
Through twilight's veil, a glimpse of light,
A dance of joy, set hearts alight.

So join the dance, let spirits lead,
In velvet fields, plant every seed.
For in the rhythm of the night,
A world awakens, pure delight.

Embrace the magic, wild and free,
In every step, your spirit see.
For in the dance beneath the stars,
You'll find the truth in who you are.

Ethereal Wisp in the Glade

In the glade where shadows twine,
An ethereal wisp does softly shine,
Whispering secrets of nights untold,
Dancing in silver, radiant and bold.

Moonlight filters through branches fair,
Casting spells upon the air,
Gentle breezes weave a tune,
Cradling dreams beneath the moon.

Step lightly, tread on mossy floor,
Where ancient spirits once did soar,
Each rustle hints a tale of yore,
In this land where echoes soar.

Glimmers of magic flicker bright,
Painting shadows with soft light,
In the heart of the woodland deep,
Lies a mystery for the brave to keep.

Embrace the wisp, let your heart soar,
In the glade where magic's at the core,
Whispers invite, a journey begins,
Where reality fades, and wonder wins.

Mirage of the Enchanted Realm

In the mirage, colors blend and weave,
An enchanted realm for those who believe,
Winds of fortune whisper through the trees,
Carrying tales on the softest breeze.

Rivers shimmer like liquid glass,
Reflecting dreams as the moments pass,
Each ripple holds a story untold,
Unlocking wonders, both new and old.

Mountains rise with majesties rare,
Guardians of secrets that linger in air,
Upon their peaks, the echoes call,
Summoning souls to dance and sprawl.

In the vale where the flowers smile,
Joy blooms freely, a magical style,
With each petal a promise, vibrant and bold,
A testament of magic forever told.

So wander forth into this dream,
Where reality and fantasy seam,
In the mirage of an enchanted land,
Where every heartbeat is gently planned.

Silence of the Twilight Grove

In the twilight grove, silence descends,
Where the whispers of nature do make amends,
Shadows elongate, embracing the light,
As stars awaken to dance in the night.

The canopy hums a lullaby sweet,
With the rustling leaves beneath silent feet,
Hidden creatures nestle in peace,
In the stillness, the world's worries cease.

Moss carpets like velvet, soft and deep,
Where ancient spirits in silence creep,
Each breath brings forth the magic anew,
Whirling softly like morning dew.

Crickets sing under the watchful moon,
Harmonizing with the night's gentle tune,
In this sacred space where time stands still,
Hearts find solace, and dreams fulfill.

So linger here, in the night's embrace,
Let the silence weave its tranquil grace,
In the twilight grove, be lost and found,
Where beauty and stillness forever abound.

Phantoms in the Elysian Mist

In the mist where phantoms roam,
Elysian whispers call you home,
Veils of fog dance upon the ground,
Carrying echoes of love profound.

Figures glide through the ethereal haze,
Guided by memory's flickering blaze,
In their presence, time sways and bends,
Bringing solace as daylight ends.

Softly, they weave through dreams untold,
Bearing stories of the brave and bold,
Each glimmer a glint of lost desire,
A comforting touch, an ancient fire.

With every heartbeat, the mist enfolds,
Stirring the heart where the past beholds,
In the Elysian glow, spirits rise,
Breathing life into forgotten skies.

So join the dance in the gathering mist,
With phantoms and shadows, none can resist,
For in the twilight where visions cease,
Lies the promise of eternal peace.

Labyrinth of Whimsy in Dimming Light

In shadows cast by whispering trees,
A maze unfolds with gentle ease.
Each turn reveals a secret glade,
Where silence weeps, and dreams are made.

The moonlight dances on silver streams,
Awakening forgotten dreams.
With every step, the heart will race,
In this enchanting, hidden space.

Forgotten tales of yesteryear,
Echo softly, drawing near.
The winding path both old and new,
Leads wandering souls to magic's brew.

A lantern glows, a flickering spark,
Guides the way through shadows dark.
In laughter's echo, hope takes flight,
In the labyrinth of dimming light.

Where whimsy reigns and wishes glide,
In twilight's arms, where secrets hide.
Step lightly now, don't lose your way,
In this realm where night meets day.

Embraces From the Realms of Fable

In forests deep where fairies play,
And starlit paths weave dreams by day.
The whispers of a gentle breeze,
Invite the heart to pause and seize.

A tapestry of ancient lore,
Awaits beyond the enchanted door.
With every tale and knowing glance,
The spirit stirs to join the dance.

Beneath the glow of candlelight,
Fables come to life at night.
The laughter of the sprites, so sweet,
Entwines the soul, makes shadows fleet.

In every nook, a story lies,
A world of wonder in disguise.
Embraces warm from realms afar,
Where dreams are born and wishes star.

So listen close with patient ear,
For magic whispers ever near.
In the embrace of fable's smile,
You wander free, if just a while.

Shrouded Realities in Whirling Dreams

In the twilight's hush, the veil unveils,
Where reality bends, and magic sails.
Shadows entwine with whispers of light,
In dreams that spin through the endless night.

Each twirling thought, a story to tell,
In lands unknown, where wonders dwell.
Through fog and mist, lost hopes arise,
In shrouded realms beneath starry skies.

The tapestry of fate unwinds,
In swirling eddies that fate reminds.
Where wishes thought to fly away,
Are caught within the heart's bouquet.

In fleeting glimpses, the heart will yearn,
For the secrets that the shadows burn.
As dreams ignite in vibrant hues,
The soul finds solace in each muse.

And when the morning claims its throne,
The threads of night, now overgrown.
Yet in the whispers of the seams,
Lies shrouded realities in whirling dreams.

Veils of Twilight in the Glade

In the heart of the wood, shadows grow,
Whispers of magic in the soft, dim glow.
Beneath ancient boughs, secrets take flight,
Veils of twilight dance in the fading light.

Moonbeams weave through a silken mist,
Every creature within it exists.
Mysteries linger, hidden and deep,
Guardians watch over what they keep.

Footsteps echo on paths overgrown,
Each rustle a tale from ages unknown.
The glade is alive with stories untold,
In twilight's embrace, their magic unfolds.

Luminous petals catch starlight's gleam,
In the hush of dusk, we stumble on dreams.
Time drifts like leaves on a whispering stream,
In the glade, all is woven in seam.

With the night as a cloak, we venture forth,
Finding solace in the secrets of Earth.
Beneath veils of twilight, we dare to roam,
In the glade's gentle arms, we find our home.

Threads of Dreams on Dewy Grass

Softly the dawn stretches across the field,
A tapestry woven, each moment revealed.
Threads of dreams shimmer on dew-kissed blades,
In this world of wonder, enchantment pervades.

Whispers of hope rise with the sun,
Each droplet a wish, a journey begun.
Colorful visions paint skies anew,
In this cradle of day, where magic is true.

Morning's embrace, gentle and bright,
Invites every heart to take flight.
Over horizons where dreams break free,
On dewy grass, we are all meant to be.

Every step taken, a story unfolds,
In this garden of wonders, where each face holds.
Laughter like petals, soft in the breeze,
Dancing with light, through branches and trees.

As noon weaves its warmth through leaves up high,
In this thread of life, we learn to fly.
With dreams intertwined, we lose and we find,
On a canvas of grass, our souls are aligned.

Flickering Hues in the Faery Night

Under the cloak of the midnight sky,
Flickering hues like stars soaring high.
Elfin laughter rings through the trees,
In faery glens where whispers tease.

Glowing lanterns float on a gentle stream,
Each flicker a secret, a soft, tender dream.
Mirrored reflections, life dancing in light,
A playground of shadows in depths of the night.

Dreamers and wanderers gather near,
To celebrate magic, to laugh without fear.
In the heart of the forest, mysteries twine,
As the fae weave their tales on the vine.

With flickers of joy, the night comes alive,
In every soft shimmer, our spirits will thrive.
We dance with the stars through the velvet expanse,
In faery night's glow, we lose ourselves in dance.

As dawn gently stirs, like a breath set free,
The hues fade to whispers, but memory weaves.
Though night may retreat, its magic remains,
In flickering hues, our hearts leave their chains.

Elusive Echoes on Shimmering Breezes

On shimmering breezes, echoes dance light,
Carrying stories woven into the night.
Whispers of past lives call softly, yet clear,
Enticing the dreamers to lean in and hear.

The songs of the skies send shivers of grace,
Filling the air with their wistful embrace.
Elusive like shadows, they twist and they twirl,
On the gentle winds, our thoughts softly swirl.

Every leaf rustles with tales from afar,
While moonlit reflections guide us like a star.
In the stillness of dusk, our hearts start to rise,
Chasing the echoes toward endless skies.

From mountains to valleys, the breezes will soar,
Gathering secrets left on the shore.
In their soft whispering, a promise we find,
Elusive echoes drift through the mind.

As night wraps us close in its silvery shroud,
We listen to voices, both humble and loud.
On shimmering breezes, where dreams take their flight,
We seek out the magic hidden in the night.

www.ingramcontent.com/pod-product-compliance
Ingram Content Group UK Ltd.
Pitfield, Milton Keynes, MK11 3LW, UK
UKHW021436290125
4349UKWH00039B/500

9 781805 641544